All I Need to Know I Learned from My Horse

All I Need to Know
I Learned from My Horse

PAMELA C. BIDDLE & JOEL E. FISHMAN

MAIN
STREET
BOOKS

DOUBLEDAY

New York   London   Toronto   Sydney   Auckland

A Main Street Book

PUBLISHED BY DOUBLEDAY

a division of Bantam Doubleday Dell Publishing Group, Inc.

1540 Broadway, New York, New York 10036

MAIN STREET BOOKS, DOUBLEDAY, and the portrayal of a building with a tree are trademarks of Doubleday, a division of Bantam Doubleday Dell Publishing Group, Inc.

Library of Congress Cataloging-in-Publication Data

Fishman, Joel E.

All I need to know I learned from my horse / by Pamela C. Biddle and Joel E. Fishman.

p.   cm.

1. Aphorisms and apothegms. 2. Horses—Quotations, maxims, etc.

I. Biddle, Pamela C. II. Title.

PN6278.H67F57   1996

818′.5402—dc20   95-26567

CIP

ISBN 0-385-48267-1

First Main Street Books Edition: October 1996

1   3   5   7   9   10   8   6   4   2

For Lincoln and Riley,

two who elevated us

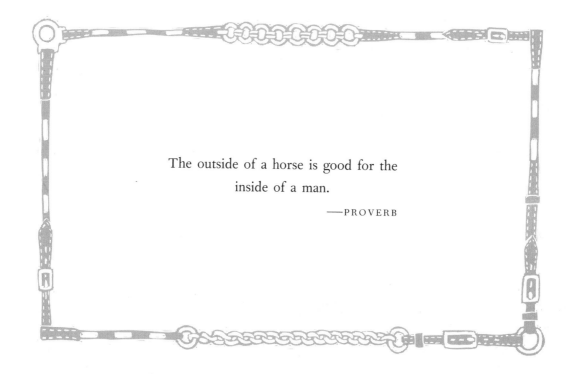

The outside of a horse is good for the
inside of a man.

——PROVERB

Introduction

The relationship between humans and horses goes back at least four thousand years, and for most of that time these majestic animals were our primary means of land transportation—after walking with our own legs, of course. Even with the refinement of the first successful gas-powered internal combustion engine in 1859, it seemed initially that horses didn't have much to worry about. After all, a horse could carry a rider across most terrain about three times faster than she could go on her own two feet. For really long distances, it could pause for a rest and a meal of grass or hay, sip some water from a stream, and be ready to continue within a matter of hours. Meanwhile the first automobiles were insanely expensive, notoriously unreliable, required frequent refueling, and did best on well-maintained roads, which most towns didn't have. And the auto couldn't even think of plowing a field, jumping a wall, pulling a cart, or chasing a cow. So you can appreciate why horses didn't see much threat to their supremacy at first.

This changed abruptly when Ford introduced the Model T in 1908. Suddenly almost everyone with a decent job could afford to go faster and in greater comfort than any horse could take them. And you didn't have to worry about your automobile running away in the middle of the night, kicking you in the head, or giving you saddle sores. You also didn't have to feed it when it wasn't working for you, and it never spooked or bucked you off, so you could usually keep your derriere out of the mud on the way to important meetings. When it rained, the roof of the car kept you dry.

Yet even as the automobile quickly diminished the horse's necessity to our daily lives, it also increased the pleasure of those who continue to ride. There are few reasons these days for most of us to employ a horse for anything but our own enjoyment, and that's just fine with most riders. It leaves us more opportunity to extend our relationship with horses in ways that our forebears seldom had time for.

Meanwhile common parlance retains strong echoes of the days when nearly everyone had a horse:

Don't look a gift horse in the mouth.

You can lead a horse to water, but you can't make him drink.

If wishes were horses, beggars would ride.

Don't put the cart before the horse.

That's a horse of a different color.

Even folks who couldn't tell a horse from a cow at thirty paces know and use these expressions of wisdom. (Of course, they also say things like "Rome wasn't built in a day," even though they never lifted a brick, which just goes to show that good aphorisms don't die easily.) The above maxims are a reminder that for those of us who still ride or own these magnificent beasts, the relationship between man and horse remains as special as it always has been. That's why horses have so much to teach us.

Sticklers (we know you're out there) who may think we are overstating the case might bridle at the idea that riding horseback offers any greater insights into life than having a pet llama would. "Horses, for all their uniqueness, just aren't that bright," they might argue stiffly. But learning from other species really has little to do with *their* IQ and lots to do with the combined wisdom of man.

As with most things in life, we don't learn so much by being told directly as we do by paying attention to subtler signs. At least half of what our parents taught us came by example, not explicit instruction. Likewise, while no real-life horse has ever whispered in anyone's ear (put your ear that close to a horse and you're likely to get bit), the discipline required of good horsemanship and the challenge of controlling a creature at least five times our size can be quite instructive.

Another way of putting this is that the world is governed by simple principles, and simple principles can carry big messages. You don't need to read Plato to know right from wrong or to learn how to get along in life. The signs are all there for those of us who choose to heed them. So it is that thousands of years after we met them, horses still have much to teach everyone about life, if you stop to think about it.

$\mathcal{K}$eep your tack clean and your britches washed.

*I*n a tug-of-war, the dumber

animal always wins.

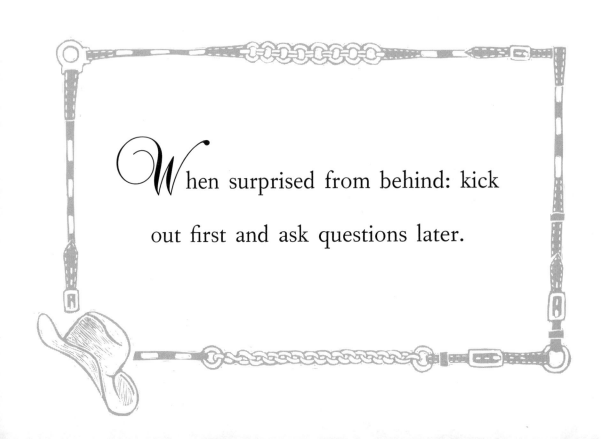

When surprised from behind: kick out first and ask questions later.

Never go out without a hat.

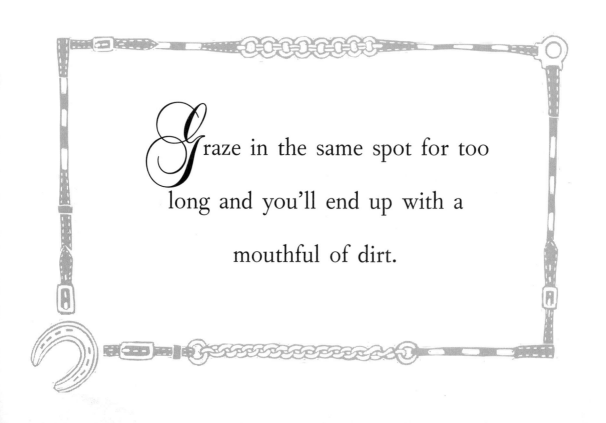

*G*raze in the same spot for too

long and you'll end up with a

mouthful of dirt.

Never end an exercise on

a bad note.

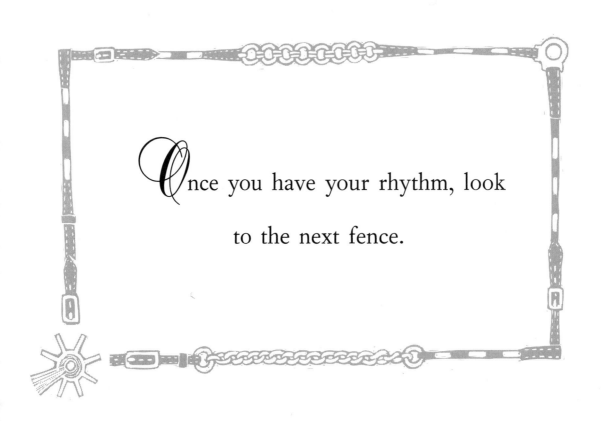

Once you have your rhythm, look
to the next fence.

Always carry a crop, but use it sparingly.

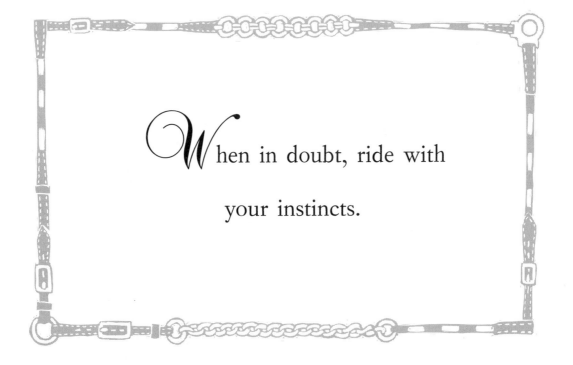

When in doubt, ride with

your instincts.

On unfamiliar terrain, stay alert

for surprises.

You don't need to gallop to

jump a cross-rail.

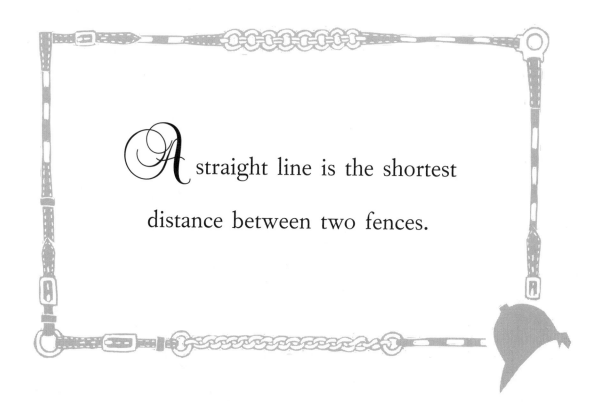

$\mathcal{A}$ straight line is the shortest

distance between two fences.

*I*f you fall off, get right back on.

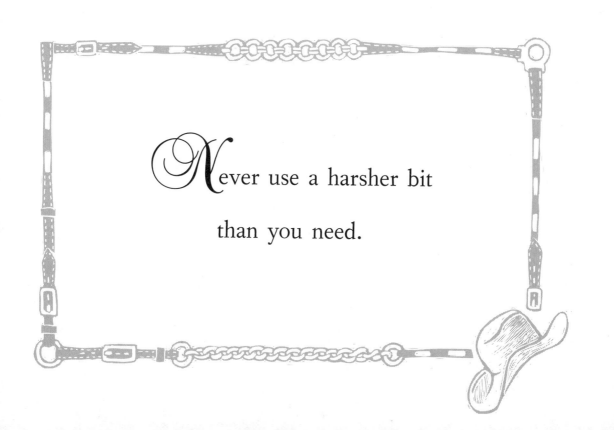

*N*ever use a harsher bit

than you need.

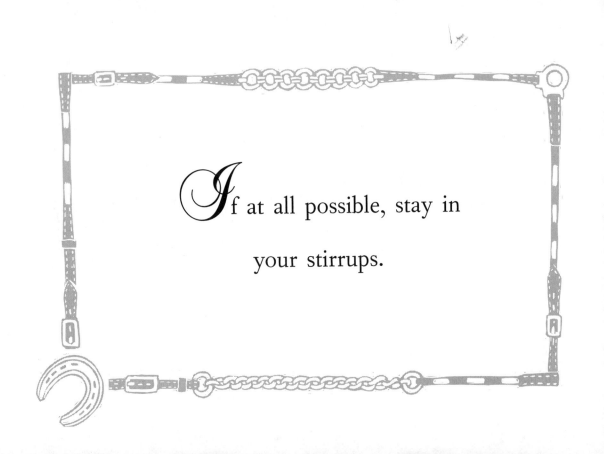

*I*f at all possible, stay in

your stirrups.

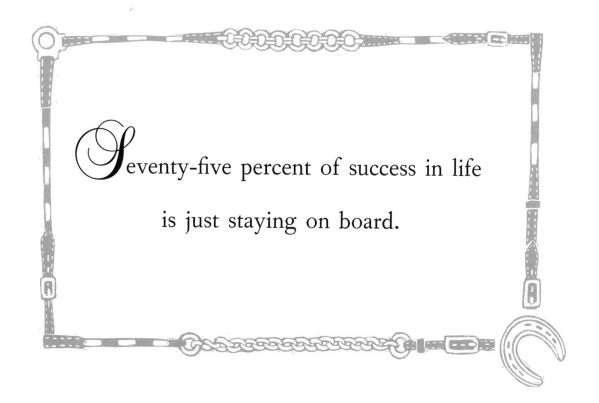

$\mathcal{S}$everty-five percent of success in life

is just staying on board.

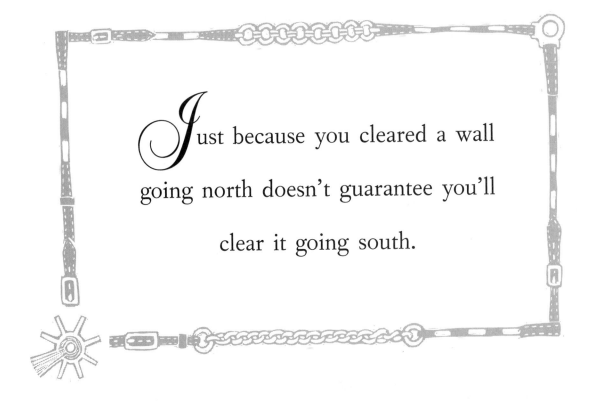

*J*ust because you cleared a wall

going north doesn't guarantee you'll

clear it going south.

$\mathcal{W}$henever possible, land feet first.

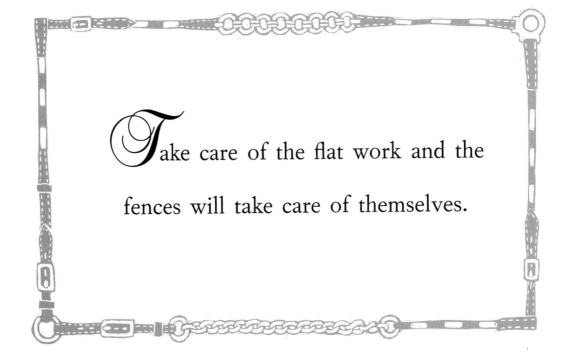

$\mathcal{T}$ake care of the flat work and the

fences will take care of themselves.

Riding well is the best revenge.

*I*n order to win, you have to run

the whole race.

Know the course before you

mount the horse.

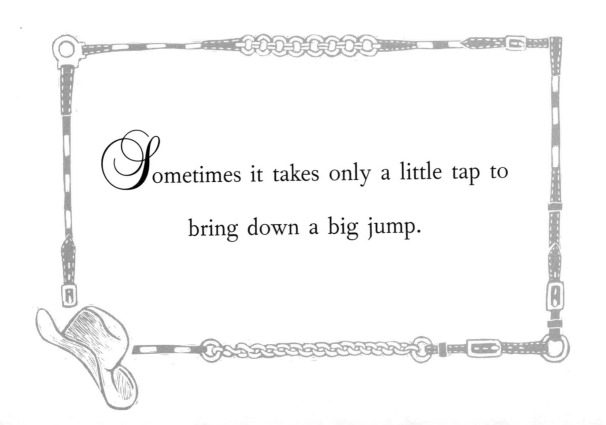

$\mathcal{S}$ometimes it takes only a little tap to

bring down a big jump.

*I*t's often the second buck

that throws you.

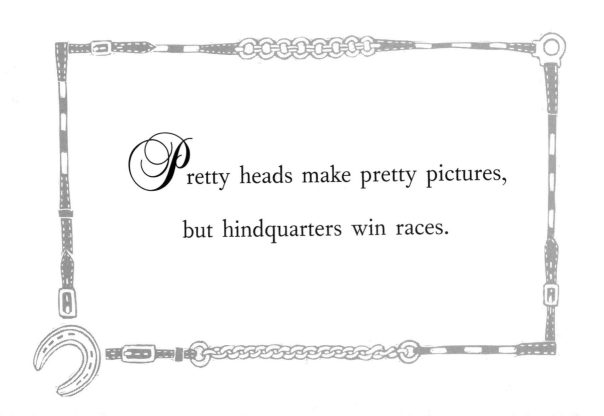

Pretty heads make pretty pictures,

but hindquarters win races.

Always sit tall in the saddle.

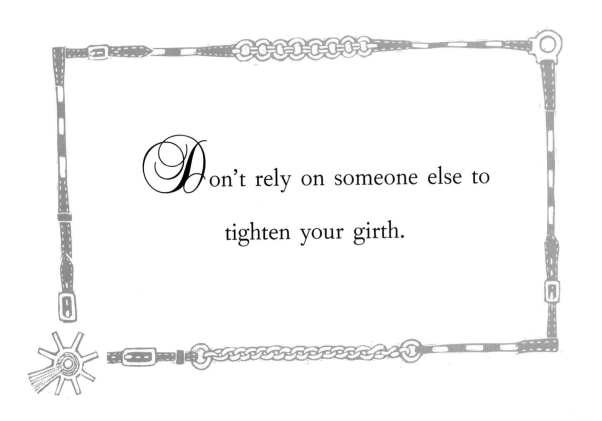

Don't rely on someone else to tighten your girth.

You can't get far on a lame horse.

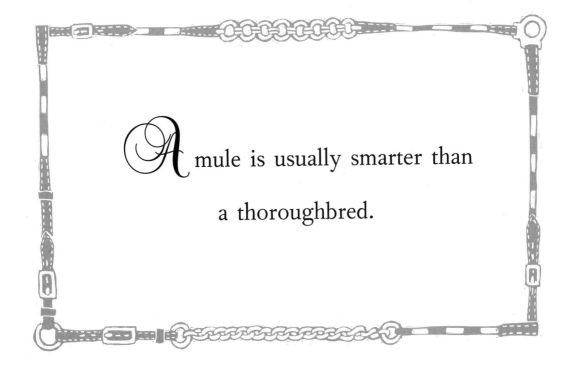

$\mathcal{A}$ mule is usually smarter than

a thoroughbred.

$\mathcal{D}$on't ride ahead of the huntsman.

When your horse paws the water,

prepare to get wet.

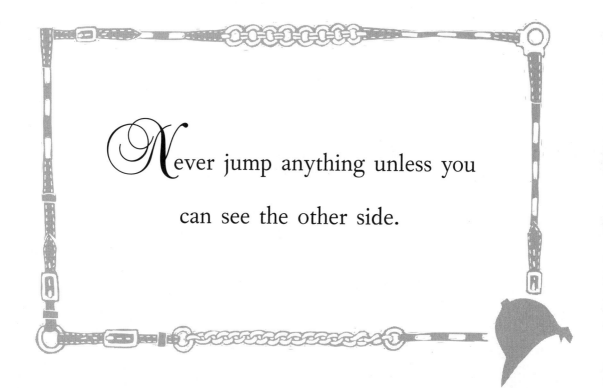

*N*ever jump anything unless you

can see the other side.

*A*lways keep a feel of your

horse's mouth.

The safest place to go is the middle of the fence.

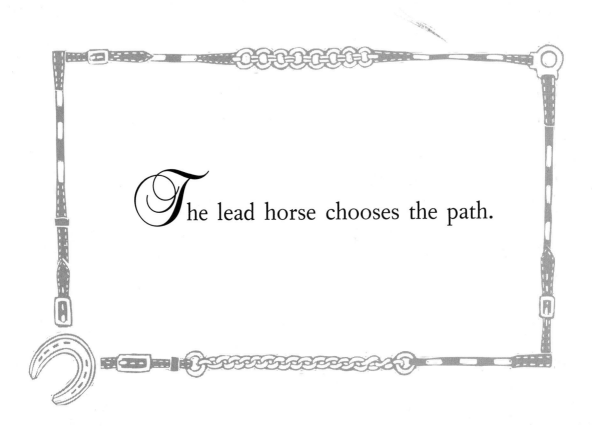

The lead horse chooses the path.

$\mathcal{K}$eep your mane pulled and your whiskers trimmed.

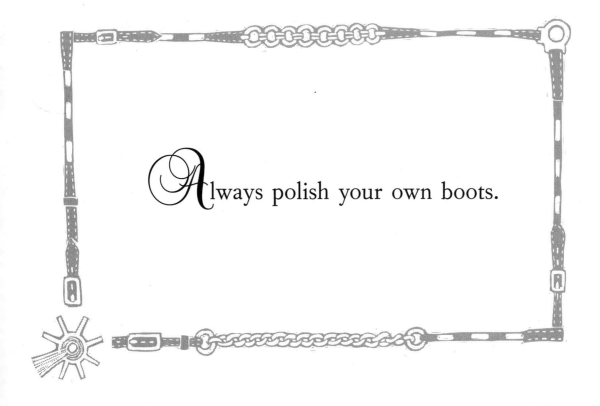

Always polish your own boots.

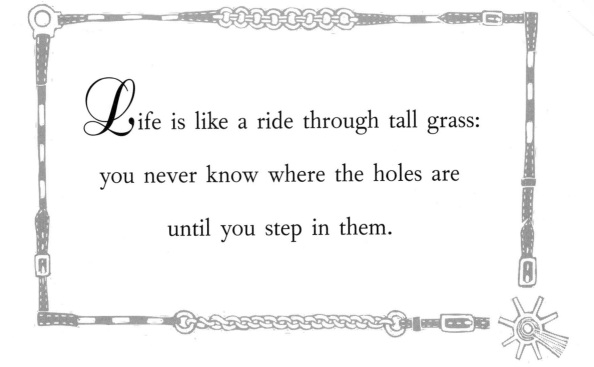

*L*ife is like a ride through tall grass:

you never know where the holes are

until you step in them.

A swish of the tail at regular

intervals keeps most pests away.

$\mathcal{N}$ever send a pony to do a

horse's job.

You have to know the jog before

you can lope.

*L*onger spurs require steadier legs—not vice versa.

Old saddles never die. They

just get cracked.

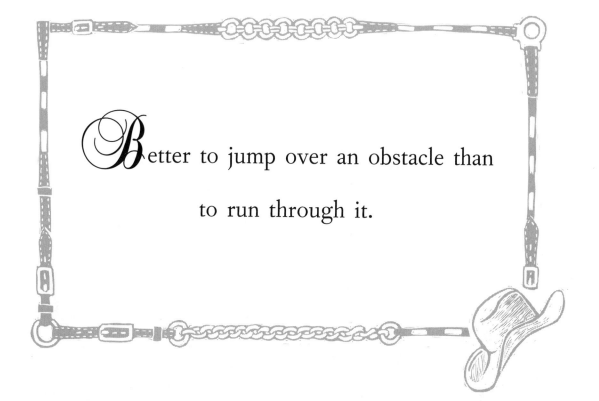

Better to jump over an obstacle than to run through it.

$\mathcal{A}$ stride in time saves nine.

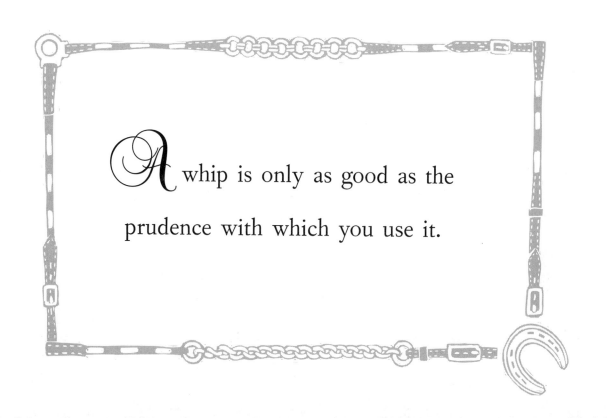

A whip is only as good as the prudence with which you use it.

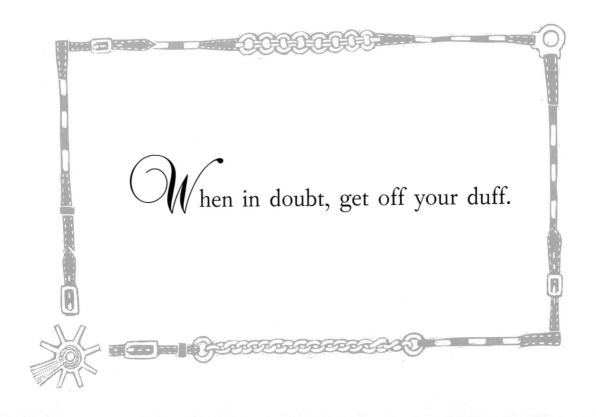

When in doubt, get off your duff.

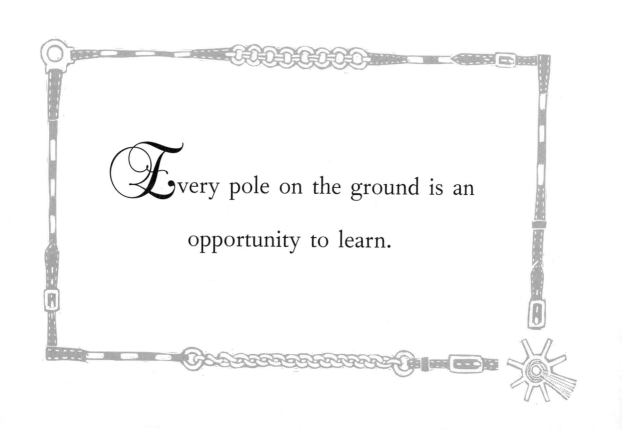

Every pole on the ground is an

opportunity to learn.

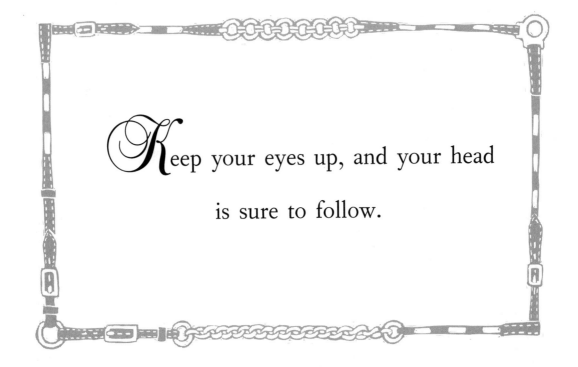

$\mathcal{K}$eep your eyes up, and your head

is sure to follow.

A good heart beats a pretty head every time.

The leg is mightier than the hand.

*W*ild oats aren't meant for sowing.

$\mathcal{I}$t takes more than talent to

win a rodeo.

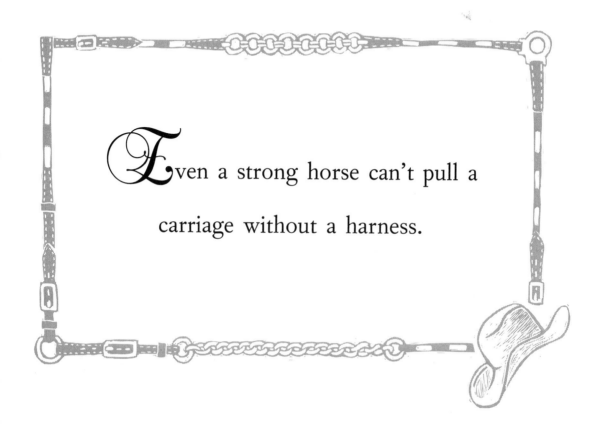

Even a strong horse can't pull a carriage without a harness.

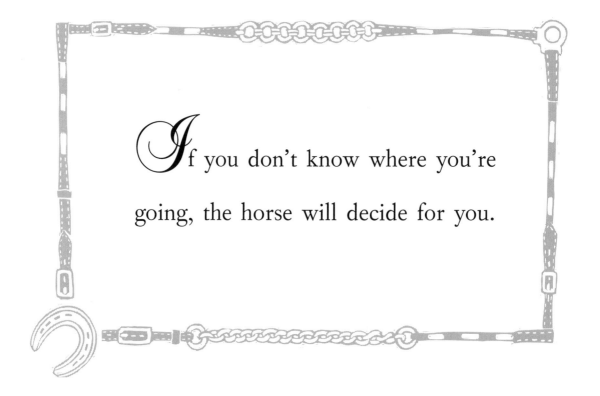

*I*f you don't know where you're going, the horse will decide for you.

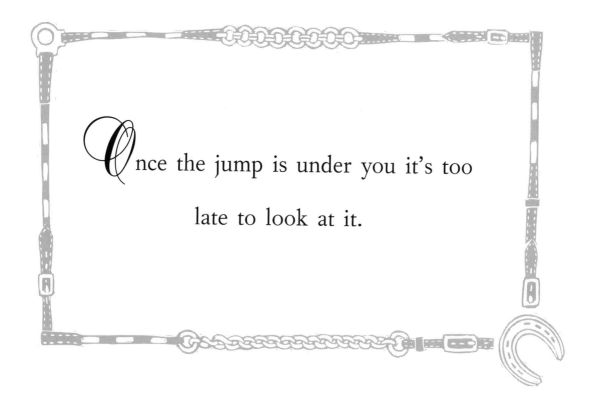

Once the jump is under you it's too

late to look at it.

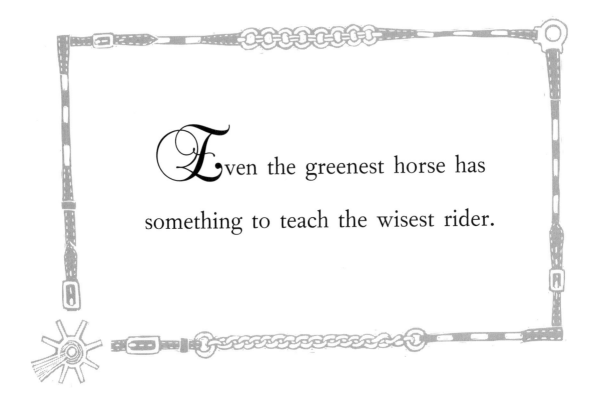

Even the greenest horse has something to teach the wisest rider.

Everything is easier when you

keep moving forward.

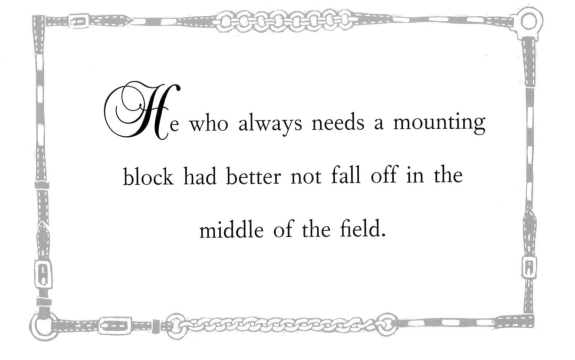

*H*e who always needs a mounting

block had better not fall off in the

middle of the field.

$\mathcal{N}$othing on four legs is quicker than

a horse heading back to the barn.

A steady hand is better than

a harsh bit.

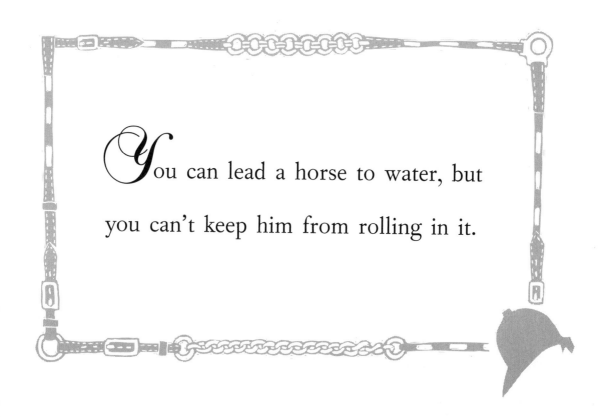

You can lead a horse to water, but you can't keep him from rolling in it.

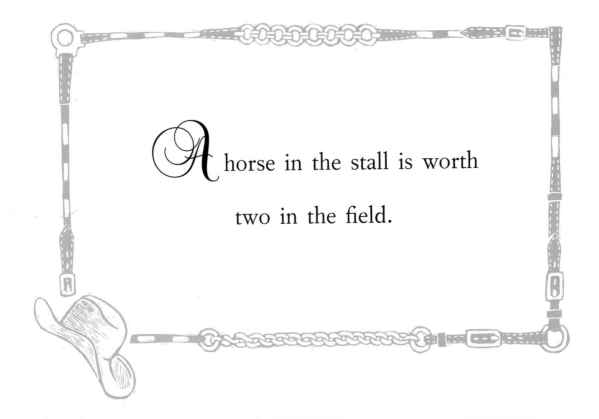

A horse in the stall is worth

two in the field.

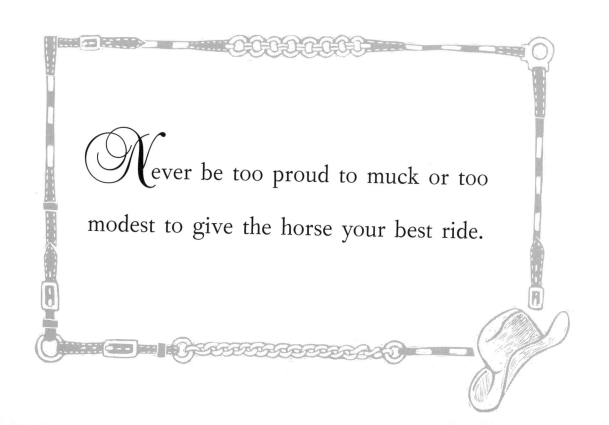

*N*ever be too proud to muck or too

modest to give the horse your best ride.

Even good judges can

have bad days.

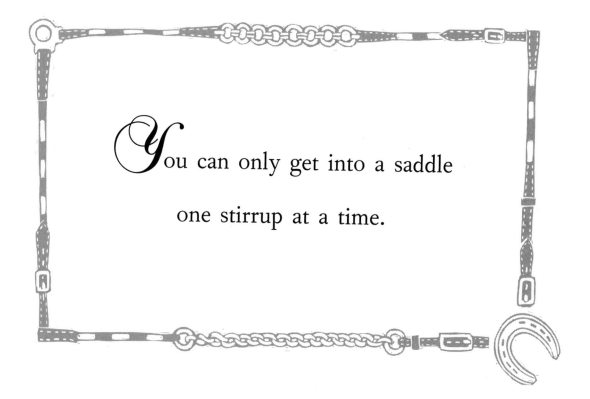

You can only get into a saddle

one stirrup at a time.

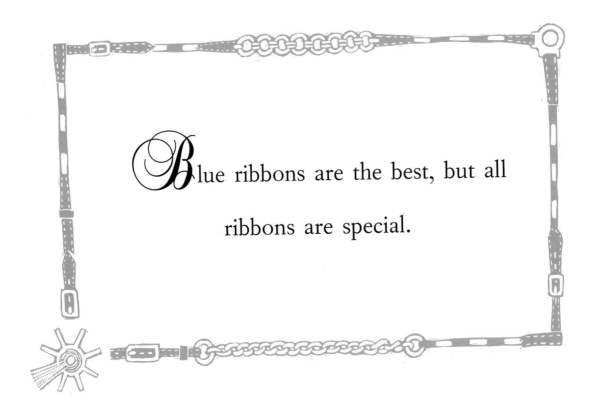

$\mathcal{B}$lue ribbons are the best, but all ribbons are special.

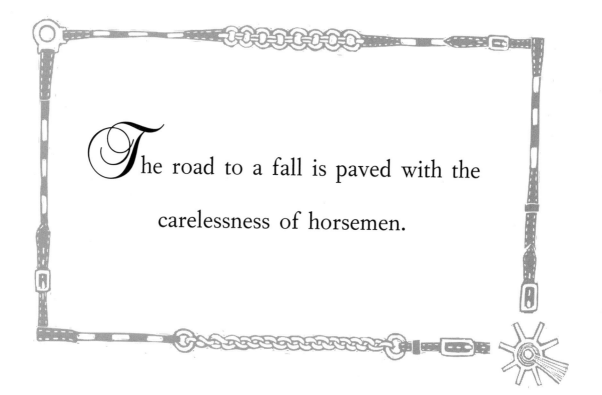

The road to a fall is paved with the carelessness of horsemen.

*L*uck favors the prepared rider.

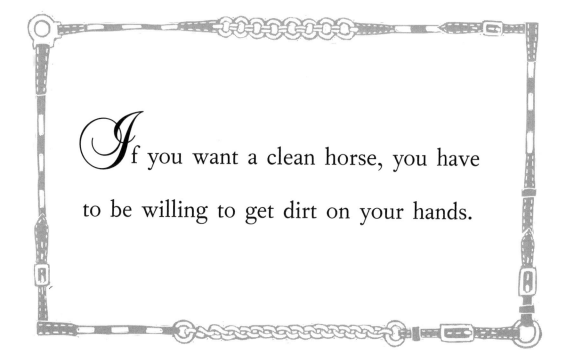

*I*f you want a clean horse, you have

to be willing to get dirt on your hands.

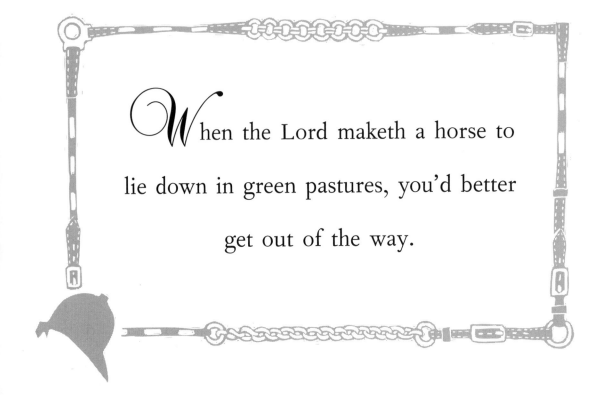

When the Lord maketh a horse to lie down in green pastures, you'd better get out of the way.

Don't judge a horse by its color.

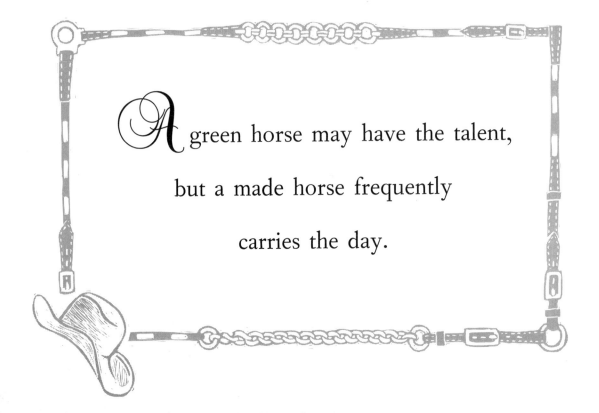

A green horse may have the talent,

but a made horse frequently

carries the day.

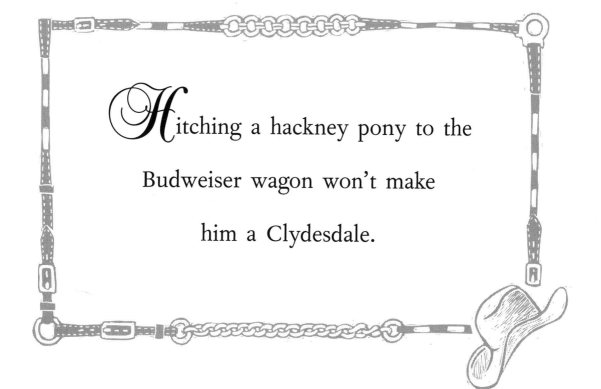

*H*itching a hackney pony to the Budweiser wagon won't make him a Clydesdale.

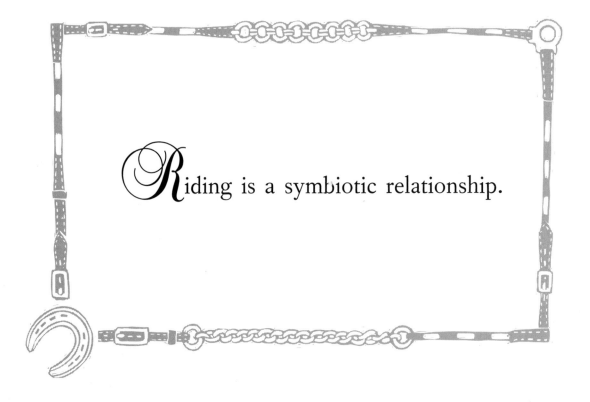

*R*iding is a symbiotic relationship.

Establishing a comfortable pace

early is the best way to guarantee

finishing with one.

$\mathcal{A}$ good demeanor isn't everything,

but it will always impress the judges.

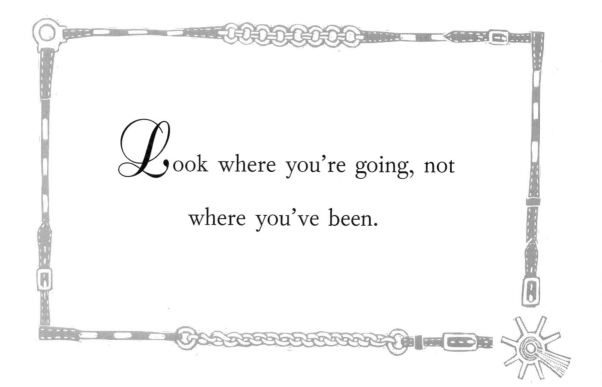

$\mathcal{L}$ook where you're going, not

where you've been.

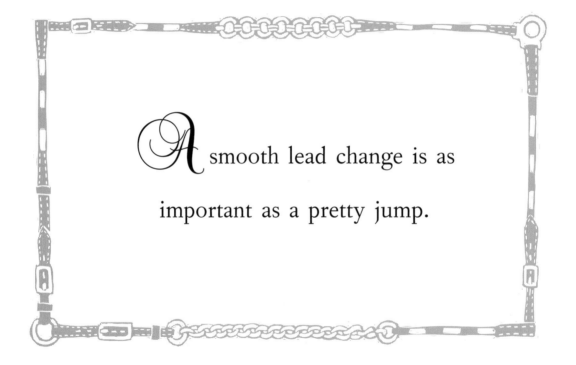

A smooth lead change is as important as a pretty jump.

$\mathcal{N}$ever let the judge see you frown.

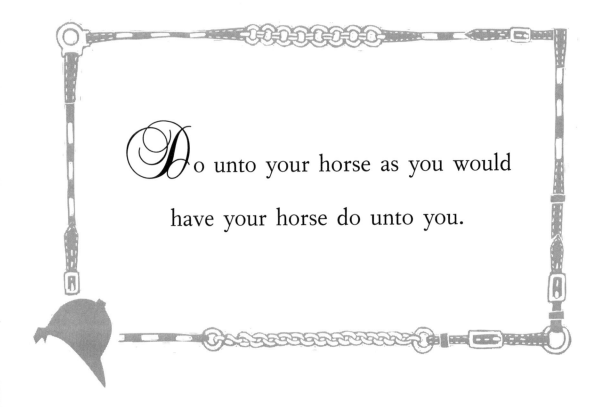

Do unto your horse as you would have your horse do unto you.

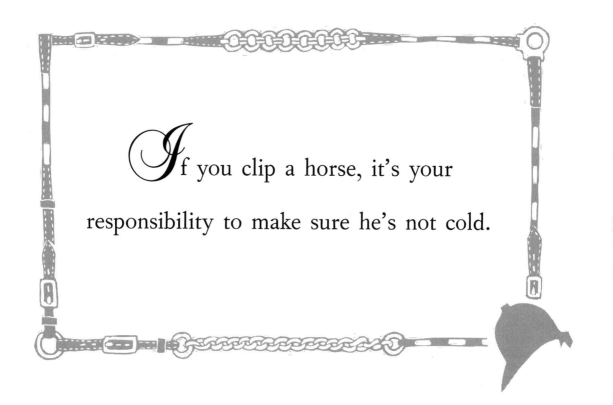

$\mathcal{I}$f you clip a horse, it's your responsibility to make sure he's not cold.

The wild horse forages his

own dinner.

*D*on't corner a frightened horse

unless you know what to do with him.

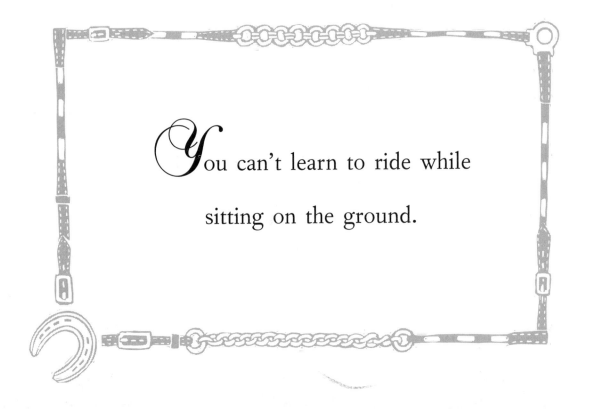

You can't learn to ride while

sitting on the ground.

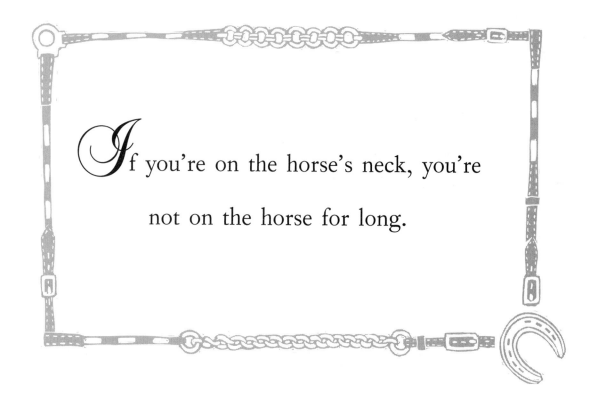

*I*f you're on the horse's neck, you're

not on the horse for long.

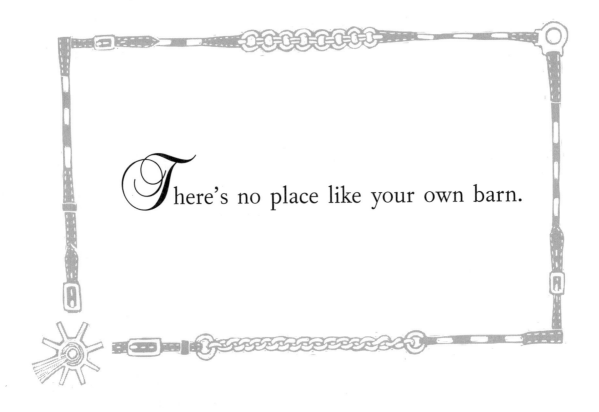

There's no place like your own barn.

$\mathcal{W}$orrying about a downed rail won't help you get to the next jump.

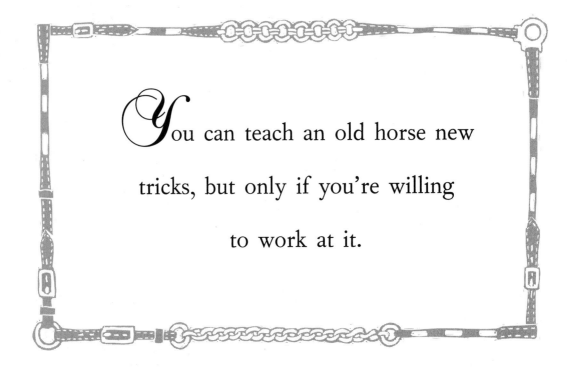

$\mathcal{Y}$ou can teach an old horse new

tricks, but only if you're willing

to work at it.

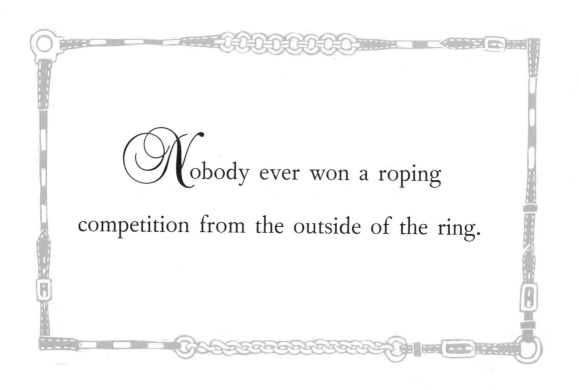

*N*obody ever won a roping

competition from the outside of the ring.

*L*ook before your horse leaps.

One rotten horse can spoil

the whole herd.

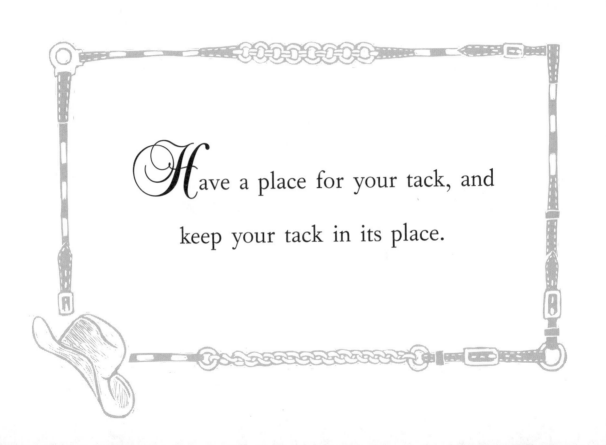

Have a place for your tack, and

keep your tack in its place.

A horse that was vetted last week

isn't guaranteed sound today.

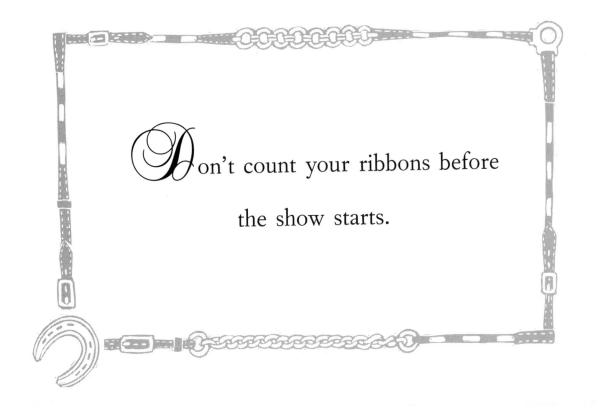

*D*on't count your ribbons before

the show starts.

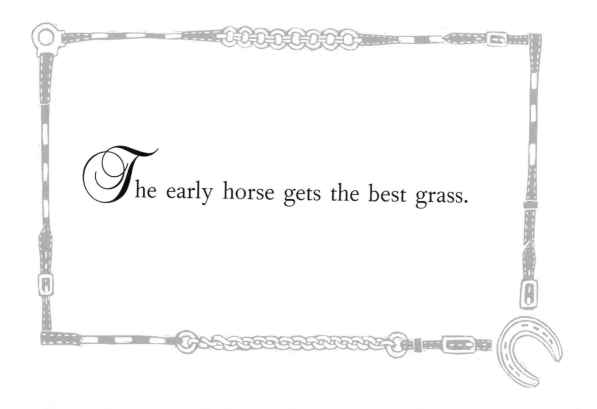

The early horse gets the best grass.

*D*on't bite the hand that feeds

you apples.

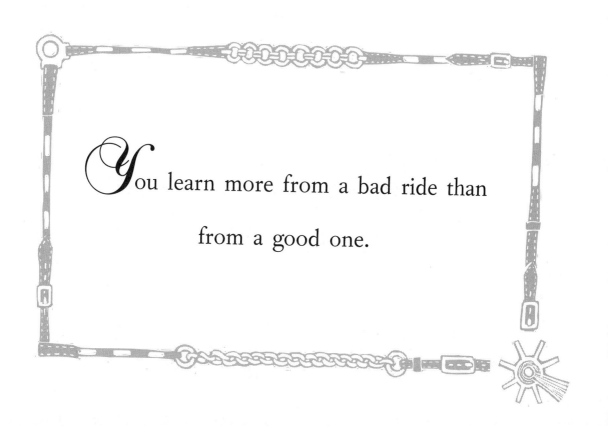

You learn more from a bad ride than from a good one.

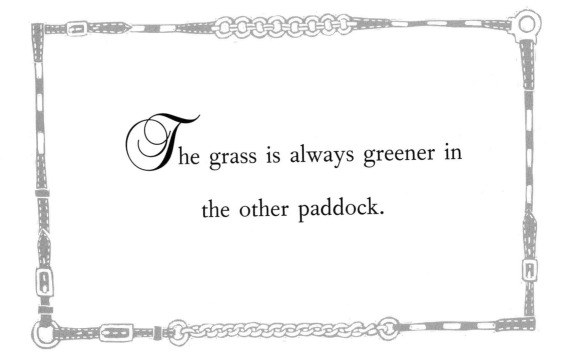

The grass is always greener in

the other paddock.

*G*reat Percherons from little

foals grow.

A penny saved is a penny you can spend on your next horse.

Horses can't talk, but they can

speak if you listen.

For want of a shoe nail, the horse goes lame.

The cross-country journey begins

with a single stride.

When in Texas, ride as the

cowboys do.

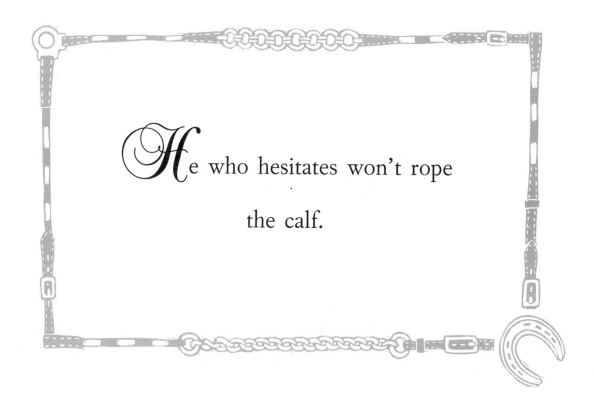

*H*e who hesitates won't rope

the calf.

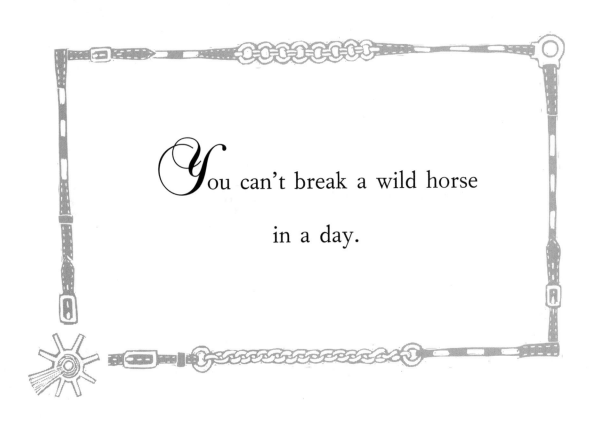

You can't break a wild horse

in a day.

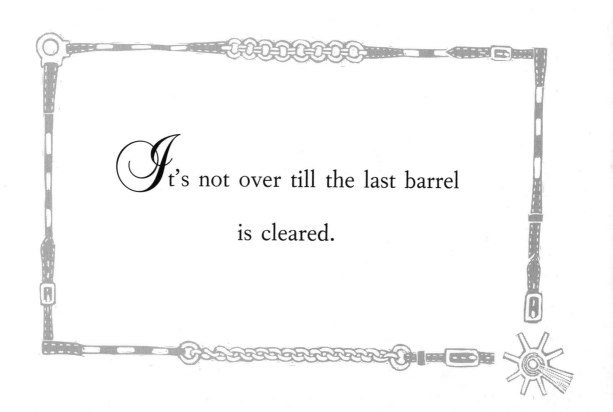

*I*t's not over till the last barrel

is cleared.

The proof of the horse is

in the riding.

There's more than one way to

cross the ring.

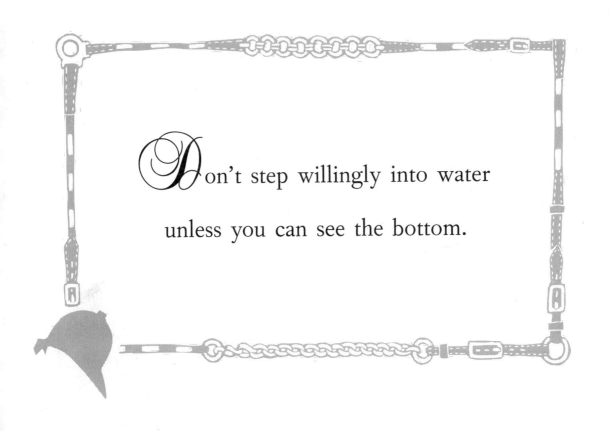

$\mathcal{D}$on't step willingly into water

unless you can see the bottom.

*D*on't crack the whip before you check the harness.

A hot horse and a hot head

don't mix.

*J*ust because a horse swims doesn't

make him a fish.

And remember: A pair of boots and chaps doesn't make you a rider.